MW00806229

A Collection of Sunday Sermons for Children

52 Weeks of Great Ideas for Parents and Teachers

GRETCHEN ARNOLD

Grace Avenue Publishing, LLC
COLORADO SPRINGS, COLORADO

Dedication

This book is dedicated
to the Glory of God,
without whom
it never could have been written!

Table of Contents

Summer

Fall

Winter

Appendix

Introduction

For several decades I have enjoyed telling children Bible stories during their Children's Sunday Sermon time at my local United Methodist Church. After accumulating hundreds of messages piled high in a box, it was time to choose a few of my favorites and write a book. This book provides new material for sharing the Bible with little ones. It is a collection of 52 messages that are perfect for the busy parent, grandparent, Children's Sunday Sermon leader, or teacher—anywhere children can hear of God's love in everyday settings and easy to understand words. With each story lasting from three to five minutes, it is concise, fun, and inspirational for adult and child.

I've always begun by welcoming the youngsters as they come forward to hear their Children's Message and thank them for coming up. OR if you are talking to your own children, remember to praise them for wanting to hear the stories of the Bible!

A scripture is included with each story, so you or a child may want to read it out loud. (Unless otherwise noted, all scripture references are from the New International Version of the Bible – NIV.) With almost all of the stories, a visual aid is suggested. You can also use something you think will capture the attention of your audience. Speak slowly and emphasize those sections underlined or in bold. Be dramatic and use good story-telling skills to involve your group. Always read the presentation a few times to become familiar with it before telling the children. Since each section is quite short, you might want to memorize it or use it as a springboard for your own words so you will not have to read it, unless you want to. Each story is complete on its own.

End your time together by asking everyone to hold hands and repeat after you in prayer. This may be their first introduction on how to pray, so begin consistently with, "Dear God, we thank you for…" and then add your own touch. End each prayer with "In Jesus' name, Amen." Sometimes I remind the children that we all hold hands because we are the family of God and this is one way that we are all connected.

Each of these stories has been used at least once in the 40 years I have presented the Children's Sunday messages, and as my young audience keeps growing up, many of my early learners are bringing their own children to church to hear the beloved stories they heard when they were little. It has been my greatest desire that children find the Bible to be fun, exciting, and a powerful friend who is always there for them! I hope you will enjoy using these messages as a way to introduce the love of God, the gift of Jesus, and the leading of the Holy Spirit.

Spring

PSALM 17:8

"Keep me as the apple of your eye; hide me in the shadow of your wings."

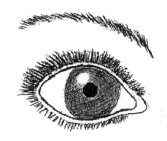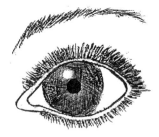

The apple of God's eye

Visual Aid: See the attached picture of two eyes.

Scripture: Psalm 17:8

When you look directly into someone's eye you see the pupil, the dark spot in the center of their eye. In Bible times, this was called the "apple of the eye."

In the above scripture, King David prayed to God, "Keep me as the apple of your eye." This meant that God was being asked to keep all of his attention on King David, as his enemies were chasing him. The second part of this scripture, "…hide me in the shadow of your wings," was a request for God to protect King David like a mother chicken protects her little chicks, close to her body in the shadow that is under her wings.

These were things that the people of the Bible understood, and now you and I understand them too! What a comforting thought it must have been for David, and is for us also, as we ask God to keep us as the apple of his eye and protect us like a mother hen protects her chicks, hidden under the shadow of her wings.

MATTHEW 6:26

*"Look at the birds of the air;
they do not sow or reap or store away
in barns, and yet your heavenly Father
feeds them. Are you not much
more valuable
than they?"*

The price of a sparrow

Visual Aid: Please see sparrow drawing in Appendix, page 124.

Scripture: Matthew 6:26

I n Bible times, two sparrows would cost a farthing, about a fourth of a penny in today's money. Sounds like there was not much value to a sparrow! And yet, have you ever looked at those little birds? They are a bundle of fluff. They are lighter than a handful of cotton balls, and yet God dresses them in lovely, soft feathers of tan and brown, and black and white; some have stripes or spots. Many have tiny, pink legs and feet.

In those days, sparrows had very little value, and yet God fed them and clothed them. Matthew 10:29 says that not one of them can fall to the ground without God knowing it. The question is, are you worth more than a handful of cotton balls, a quarter of a penny, or a bundle of fluff? Yes, you are! God says you are. So, if sparrows are fed and clothed by God, then certainly you and I, who are much more valuable than sparrows, will be cared for by God too. Food and clothing and everything you need will be supplied when you seek God first.

"Go to the great city of Nineveh
and preach against it, because its
wickedness has come up before me.
But Jonah ran away from the Lord
and headed for Tarshish."

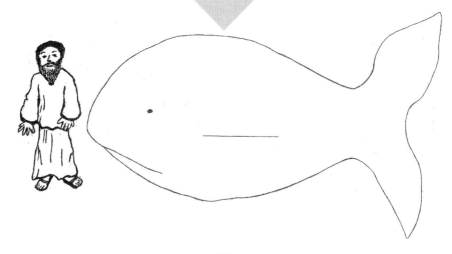

Time out for Jonah

Visual Aid: See the whale/Jonah picture in the Appendix, page 125.

Scripture: Jonah 1:2-3a

Have you ever had a time-out when your parents or teachers told you to go sit quietly somewhere and think about what you just said or did? This idea of having a time-out is very old. In fact, that is what God did with his prophet, Jonah. God told Jonah to go and preach to the city of Nineveh (which was a very wicked place with violent people) and tell them to repent and turn from their evil ways or God would destroy them! Jonah was probably afraid, so he said NO and ran away.

Jonah ran away and jumped in a boat that was headed for a different city, when a big storm came up and Jonah was washed over the side of the boat. But God had prepared a whale, and when Jonah fell out of the boat, the big whale swallowed him right up! God had put Jonah in time-out! Jonah had to sit in the whale's tummy and think about how he had disobeyed God.

Jonah sat there for three days and three nights in that stinky seawater with seaweed on his head and dead fish sloshing around his feet and thought about what he had done! Finally, Jonah realized that he had to obey God and go where God was sending him.

Sometimes we don't want to do what our parents or teachers tell us to do, but we are supposed to obey God, and God says that children are to obey their parents. So even if you don't want to do what your parents or teachers tell you to do, it is best to obey and do what you are told to do. That way you don't have to sit in a corner, or go to your room, or worse yet, sit in a whale's belly!

MATTHEW 4:4

"Jesus answered, 'It is written:
Man shall not live on bread alone,
but on every word that comes from
the mouth of God.'"

Rocks and Rolls 4

Visual Aid: Give each child a small roll to eat.

Scripture: Matthew 4:4

Restaurants want you to eat their dinner rolls before your dinner comes, so they tempt you by offering warm, soft dinner rolls that smell so good!

There is a story in the Bible where the devil tempts Jesus to turn stones into bread. The story goes like this: Jesus was led by the Holy Spirit into the wilderness to be tempted by the devil.

After 40 days and 40 nights without food, Jesus was very hungry! There were many rocks around where Jesus was, and the devil came to Jesus and said, "If you are the Son of God, tell these stones to become bread."

Jesus could have done that, and he was very hungry. So why didn't he change the rocks into bread? Because the devil was tempting Jesus to take care of his own needs instead of trusting God to take care of him. Jesus knew that God his Father would take care of him. So Jesus answered the devil by saying, "It is written, Man shall not live on bread alone, but on every word that comes from the mouth of God."

Jesus knew this verse, which comes from Deuteronomy 8:3, because he had learned many scriptures as he was growing up.

It is important that you learn scriptures too, so when you are tempted, you will have God's word right in your mind to help you be strong and not give in to temptation!

19

JOHN 4:10 NLT

"Jesus replied,
'If you only knew the gift
God has for you and who you are
speaking to, you would ask me,
and I would give you
living water.'"

Living Water 5

Visual Aid: Provide each child with a small bottle of water or a cup of water.

Scripture: John 4:10 NLT

One hot afternoon Jesus was thirsty, so he sat down by a well in the country of Samaria. As he was resting, a woman came along to get water from the well, so Jesus asked her for a drink. She was shocked because in that day, Jewish MEN did not speak to strange women and certainly not to a Samaritan woman! Jesus told her if she knew who he was, she would ask him for the living water so she would never be thirsty again.

That caught the woman's attention. Every day she had to walk to the well by herself and haul water back to her house, so she wanted to know all about Jesus' living water.

Jesus was not talking about being thirsty for regular water, however. He was talking about being thirsty for God. Jesus was telling her that there is a deep thirst in our soul for God, and God is that living water Jesus was talking about.

So, the next time you have a drink of water, remember that your soul is as thirsty for God as your mouth is thirsty for cool water on a hot day. Ask Jesus into your heart so that special kind of thirst is taken care of!

MATTHEW 23:37

"...how often I have longed
to gather your children together,
as a hen gathers her chicks under her
wings, and you were not willing."

Hens and Chicks 6

Visual Aid: Use a picture of mother hen or use the drawing in
the Appendix, page 126.

Scripture: Matthew 23:37

In Jesus' day, every family had chickens. One day, when Jesus was talking to a group of people, he used a mother hen for an example. He said that when there was danger, the hen would spread her wings out so the chicks could run for cover under their mother's protective wings!

Jesus told the people he had often wanted to gather them together just like a mother hen and protect them. Even though the people understood this idea, they would not listen to Jesus' idea. We don't know why they didn't listen to Jesus. Maybe they didn't understand that he was God's Son and that he really could protect them.

Today, however, we have the Bible to help us understand who Jesus is and how much he loves us and wants to protect us. We can trust him just like little chicks trust the mother hen.

Pray that God will give you understanding when you hear Bible stories being read to you! Then you will understand what Jesus means.

JOHN 21:15

"When they had finished eating, Jesus said to Simon Peter, 'Simon son of John, do you love me more than these?' 'Yes, Lord,' he said, 'you know that I love you.'"

John 21:15

**Jesus said,
Do you love me?**

John 21:15

**Yes Lord, you know
that I love you**

After Breakfast 7

Visual Aid: Show children a heart with Jesus' words on one side and Peter's on the other side. Directions are in the Appendix, page 127.

Scripture: John 21:15

Jesus may have asked Peter three times because, before this, Peter had denied knowing Jesus three times.

Peter was sorry; he needed forgiveness, and Jesus knew that! Since Peter had said he didn't know Jesus three different times, now Peter got to say to Jesus, "Lord you know I love you," three times.

Since Jesus knows everything we do, when we do something wrong he wants us to come to him for forgiveness. So, when you do something wrong, don't fuss about it and hold on to the bad feelings. Go to Jesus and ask for forgiveness and then, as Peter did, tell Jesus you love him. You will feel so much better!

"*We love
because he [God]
first loved us.*"

Elephants Remember

Visual Aid: Copy the elephant picture in the Appendix, page 128, for each child.

Scripture: 1 John 4:19

Wild elephants learn to find food and water by following their mothers, aunts, and others in their herd. Elephants remember these lessons even when they are very old. They learn to follow the same old trails that elephants have traveled for many, many years, and they remember!

When one elephant gently rubs a younger elephant's back with her trunk or helps it up a hill, that young elephant remembers how to love her own baby in the very same way.

Elephants remember that special kind of care and affection, and they pass it on because they were loved first. People learn in much the same way; perhaps we learn this love from our family, but that isn't the only way. The scripture tells us that we love because God first loved us!

All around us, we see how God teaches us to love one another. God first showed his love for us by sending his only begotten Son, Jesus, so we will know how to love.

God gives us elephants as an example of how to care for one another, and Jesus is our example of how to love.

1 SAMUEL 1:27

"I prayed for this child, and the Lord has granted me what I asked of him."

Hang on to your dreams 9

Visual Aid: Have a picture of a firefighter, athlete etc.

Scripture: 1 Samuel 1:27

Do you have a dream of what you want to be when you grow up? God knows what you like to do and what you are good at. So don't give up. Ask God to help you with that dream.

There is a story in the Bible about a lady named Hannah who wanted to have a baby. Although she prayed for this year after year, no baby came to her and her husband. Finally, Hannah went to the temple to pray for a baby, only this time she told God that if she could have a son, she would give her boy to God and take him to the temple to live and learn about God.

Hannah's dream came true! Her prayers were answered. She named her son Samuel, which means gift from God. Samuel grew up learning about God, became a leader among God's people, and did many wonderful things in his life. As for Hannah, she had several other children after Samuel. She dreamed of having one child, and her prayers were answered with even more children!

Ask God what he wants for your life and, like Hannah, you too can be blessed!

PSALM 98:4 KJV

*"Make a joyful noise
unto the Lord, all the earth:
make a loud noise, and rejoice,
and sing praise."*

Make a joyful noise 10

Visual Aid: Small rocks or sand in a closed cardboard tube makes a joyful noise when tipped.

Scripture: Psalm 98:4 KJV

Have you heard the birds singing these last few days? It is spring! The scripture today tells us that all the earth is to make a loud noise and rejoice and sing praise to the Lord.

Birds can't read, but they sure know how to praise the Lord with song! You and I are also told to praise the Lord with songs and joyful noise, just like the birds do.

In the neighborhood, some children were making their own music by using paper cups with straws that squeaked as the straws went up and down in the lids. Some other children were blowing into bottles, and another child was banging on a trash can lid. Still others were clapping their hands or singing.

It was a beautiful noise; it was joyful music. We can't all sing like birds, but we can make a joyful noise to the Lord, and we can sing praises unto the Lord our God! Can you think of other ways that the earth makes a joyful noise? (Wind in the leaves, water rushing down a stream, frogs croaking, crickets singing, thunder…)

JEREMIAH 18:4 NLT

"But the jar he was making did not turn out as he had hoped, so he crushed it into a lump of clay and started over."

Oops! ◆ 11

Visual Aid: Beforehand, make the soft clay recipe in the Appendix, page 129.

Scripture: Jeremiah 18:4 NLT

Jeremiah was a man of God, a prophet, who traveled around teaching people God's word. One day God was telling Jeremiah about a potter who made pots of clay.

When one of the clay pots was dented as the potter was working on it, the potter stopped and squashed the clay back together in a lump and started again to make a nice new bowl or jug out of the same clay. God said His people were like the clay.

When they did something wrong, if they asked for forgiveness, God would start all over again with them and make them better people. Like the potter, God does not give up; he simply begins again and will forgive the wrong things his people do when they ask for forgiveness. Then, like the potter's new jug or bowl, God's people are even better than what they were before.

MATTHEW 13:55 and 56a

"Isn't this the carpenter's son?
Isn't his mother's name Mary, and
aren't his brothers James, Joseph, Simon
and Judas? Aren't all his
sisters with us?"

Blended Families 12

Visual Aid: Show pictures of blended families.

Scripture: Matthew 13:55 and 56a

There are many blended families in our world who now live together as a whole family. Jesus belonged to one such family. His mother, Mary, had four other sons and some daughters too. The father of these children was Joseph, Mary's husband. So, Jesus lived in a blended family too. Jesus was Mary's first son, and his father was God.

James, Joseph, Simon, and Judas were his little brothers, and he had some sisters too, and although we don't know their names, we can be sure Jesus loved his little sisters too.

If you have brothers and sisters from another mother or father living in your family, you share that special connection with Jesus. Congratulations! Jesus lived in a blended family, and he knows all about what you are going through as you join together to form a whole family.

Ask Jesus to bless your new brothers and sisters and to help and guide you into loving each other. Then remember to thank God for sending Jesus to show us how to love all of our brothers and sisters.

ROMANS 10:15

*"How beautiful
are the feet of those who
bring good news!"*

(SEE ALSO ISAIAH 57:7
and NAHUM 1:15)

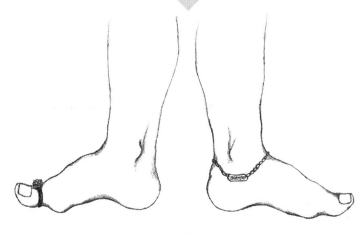

Your beautiful feet 13

Visual Aid: Find a friend who will show the children their painted toenails or use the picture in the Appendix, page 130.

Scripture: Romans 10:15

Take a good look at someone's feet. Feet may not be the prettiest part of the body, but the Bible doesn't say, beautiful are the feet with painted toenails, or beautiful are the feet with rings on their little toes, or beautiful are the feet in pretty sandals. It says feet are beautiful when they bring good news.

So, what is the good news our feet are to bring? What makes even our feet beautiful?

The Bible says in Romans 10:15 (and again in Isaiah 57:7 and Nahum 1:15), that those who bring the good news of peace and salvation are those people with the beautiful feet. When we bring the good news that God sent his son Jesus as the Savior for all people, and when we tell other people of the peace that fills our heart, then we, too, have those beautiful feet that the Bible talks about because we are bringing the good news.

Summer

MATTHEW 5:16 KJV

"Let your light so shine before men, that they may see your good works, and glorify your Father which is in heaven."

Practice what you're good at

Visual Aid: Show a light bulb, or a picture of one.

Scripture: Matthew 5:16 KJV

Thomas Edison invented the first light bulb, and it was made the same way for over 130 years! Thomas Edison tried many times before he was able to make the light bulb work. He didn't get up one morning and TADA! make a light bulb. No, it took him a long time and over 5,000 tries to get it right. But because he loved inventing, he kept at it until he made a light bulb that worked.

God gives each one of us something that we do very well. But like Mr. Edison, we need to work at it to make it better. Those who can sing need to keep on singing; those who draw need to keep on drawing; those who are kind need to be kind all the time.

Each of us is given something that we like to do, so whatever that is, keep working on it until you become very good at it! We glorify God by doing what we like to do and doing it well. So keep practicing at what you are good at and give God the glory!

DEUTERONOMY 31:6 KJV

"Be strong and of a good courage, fear not, nor be afraid of them: for the Lord thy God, he it is that doth go with thee; he will not fail thee nor forsake thee."

The parachute packer

Visual Aid: See directions for making a plastic bag parachute
in the Appendix, page 131.

Scripture: Deuteronomy 31:6 KJV

One day there was a skydiver who jumped out of an airplane. The parachute opened up and the person floated gently to the ground.

Who packed that parachute? Only someone who knew how to do this correctly could have packed the parachute. If it was not packed correctly, it would fail and the parachute would not open when it should. The person who trusted that parachute to open could be hurt in a fall so it is very, very important that the parachute is folded perfectly.

That reminds us of a scripture in the Bible when Moses was telling God's people that God would go with them and not fail them or leave them. The people of the Bible trusted God to be with them, and since God is the same today as he was in Bible times, God can be trusted today! God is like the expert parachute packer. God can be trusted; he will not fail you, ever.

MATTHEW 4:19

*"Come, follow me,"
Jesus said, "and I will
send you out to fish
for people."*

Gone fishing 16

Visual Aid: Offer fish shaped crackers as a good treat.

Scripture: Matthew 4:19

Jesus was looking for disciples who would follow him to learn about God. One day Jesus saw two brothers who were casting their nets out into the sea because they were fishermen, and Jesus called out to them saying, "Come, follow me, and I will make you fishers of men!"

Now that was an interesting idea! The two men, Andrew and his brother Simon Peter, made their living catching fish, all kinds of fish. All different kinds of fish were caught in the fishermen's nets—big fish, small fish, long skinny fish, and short round fish. These men understood they might catch all different shapes and sizes of people—men and women, old and young, tall and short! These two brothers and ten other men joined Jesus to become fishers of men because Jesus wanted to bring all people to God, and these twelve men would be his fishermen. Are you ready to fish for people to bring to Jesus? You can do this by telling your friends about Jesus. Or perhaps you are one of the fish being brought to Jesus to learn about God. Fish or fisherman, remember that Jesus said, "Come and follow me."

"Remember this, a farmer who plants only a few seeds will get a small crop. But the one who plants generously will get a generous crop."

46

Johnny Appleseed 17

Visual Aid: Have an apple picture or a piece of apple to share.

Scripture: 2 Corinthians 9:6 NLT

There was a man named John Chapman who was born in 1774. John was a missionary who loved God and spread God's word everywhere he went. Although John was not rich, he wanted to do something special for God, and one day when he was eating an apple, he decided what he would do. He would plant apple trees! One apple tree will give you some apples, but if there are many apple trees, you will get lots and lots of apples.

People and animals would enjoy the fruit, God would be honored, and John would be very happy! From then on John Chapman became known as Johnny Appleseed, and he planted apple seeds all throughout the states of Pennsylvania, Ohio, Indiana, and parts of West Virginia during the 70 years that he wandered the countryside telling others about God.

Apple trees grew wherever Johnny went and for many years, tired, hungry travelers would stop beside one of those apple trees and find something to eat and a place to rest in the shade. All because John Chapman wanted to do something special for God!

Like Johnny Appleseed, we don't need to be rich to do things for God. Getting together with other kids and picking up litter that has blown into the yard is just one way to do something special for God. Maybe you can think of other things too.

GALATIANS 6:9

*"Let us not become weary
in doing good, for at the proper time
we will reap a harvest if we do not
give up."*

Don't give up 18

Visual Aid: Using a toothpick, let a child try to stab grapes.

Scripture: Galatians 6:9

There is a very tall, blue and gray bird with super long legs and a long narrow beak, called a Great Blue Heron, and it eats fish. This bird will stand in water for hours and watch for fish to come by, then it stabs its beak quickly into the water and catches a fish to eat. This may sound easy, but the Great Blue Heron may try 20 or more times before it catches a single fish.

What would happen if he became discouraged and gave up after 19 attempts? He might starve! But God made herons to have lots of patience. The Great Blue Heron doesn't give up; he keeps trying until he catches his food, and by doing that, he teaches us how to be patient! The scripture today tells us not to give up and not to become discouraged in doing good.

So even when we are working hard at something, and it doesn't seem like we will ever get the job done, don't give up! Ask God to help you, and, as God helps Great Blue Herons, God will help you, too. Just don't give up, and remember to thank God for his help.

"Now you are the body of Christ, and each one of you is a part of it."

Puzzle pieces for you

Visual Aid: See the information about making a puzzle in the Appendix, page 132.

Scripture: 1 Corinthians 12:27

Have you ever put a puzzle together? It's fun to fit all the little pieces into one big picture that looks great when you are done! What would happen if some of the puzzle pieces were not there?

It would be very upsetting, and it would be very hard to work the puzzle, wouldn't it? Imagine how it would look if you didn't have the piece that showed you a bird's body or had only a wing piece— you would never know what kind of bird it was.

This makes us think of the scripture in the Bible that tells us we are all part of Christ's body. AND, we are separate and necessary. Each one of us is important to the whole group of people who believe in God and are called the body of Christ.

So, no matter if you are young or old, big or small, you are necessary; you are important! You are the puzzle piece that holds the whole picture together. You are an important part of the body of Christ. Hooray for you, and hooray for Jesus, who loves and needs each of us!

MATTHEW 10:40

"Anyone who welcomes you welcomes me, and anyone who welcomes me, welcomes the one who sent me."

Welcome, Welcome, come on in

Visual Aid: Bring a welcome mat to place by the children.

Scripture: Matthew 10:40

The mat on the porch by the front door is what people stand on. It is the first thing they see even before they knock or ring the doorbell. This mat is very common and is known as a welcome mat in stores all across the country, and most people just wipe their feet on it.

When we go visiting with our family or friends and come to a door that has a welcome mat, as Christians, we need to remember to show the person on the other side of the door what Jesus is like.

That welcome mat is more than something to just wipe your feet on. Of course, we don't ever go up to a stranger's door, but when we go to Grandma's door or to our friend's door, then we need to remember to act like Jesus would have.

For the scripture says if they welcome us, then they also welcome Jesus, and anyone who welcomes Jesus, welcomes God!

JOHN 6:19-20

*"When they [the disciples]
had rowed about three or four miles,
they saw Jesus approaching the boat,
walking on the water; and they were
frightened. But he said to them,
'It is I; don't be afraid.'"*

Who is it? 21

Visual Aid: Share a picture of a sailing ship.

Scripture: John 6:19-20

It had been a long day for Jesus and his disciples. Jesus wanted to have some alone time, so he climbed up a mountain to pray. When it started to get dark, the disciples went down to the seashore and got into a ship to sail across the sea.

They had rowed about three or four miles when all of a sudden a great wind came up and tossed the ship around. Looking across the sea, they saw what looked like a ghost walking toward them! They were very afraid until a voice called out to them and said, "It is I; don't be afraid."

They went from being scared to now feeling, oh so safe! How wonderful it must have been to know that this was their Jesus, their very own Jesus, who had shown them miracles and taught them all about God, now walking toward them on the water! Can you imagine how relieved they must have felt? They reached their hands out to Jesus, helped him into the ship, and immediately they were safely on the far shore.

When you are afraid or something scares you, trust Jesus. Jesus tells us, "Don't be afraid. I am here, I will take care of you."

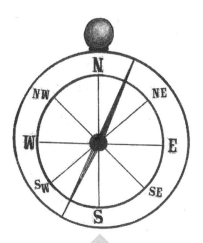

JOHN 14:6

"Jesus answered,
'I am the way, and the truth,
and the life…'"

Which way do we go? 22

Visual Aid: See the Ten Commandments in Exodus 20:3-17.

Scripture: John 14:6

In the summer, we often hear of people getting lost while hiking or climbing in the mountains. But if a hiker has a map or a guide to show him how to get out of the mountains, there is no fear of getting lost! Life sometimes can be like hiking in the mountains. It can be confusing and hard to know which way to go. We need some directions on what we should do, and God, who knows all things, gives us help so we can know which way to go.

The Ten Commandments are God's rules and help us know how to live. These rules tell us what we should do and what we shouldn't do, and just in case that isn't enough, we have God's own Son, Jesus, who shows us how to live. Like the hiker who has a map and a guide, we too have our map: God's Ten Commandments, and our guide, Jesus, to show us how to live so we will know which way to go.

MARK 1:21-22

*"They went to Capernaum
and when the Sabbath came, Jesus
went into the synagogue and began to teach.
The people were amazed at his teaching,
because he taught them as one
who had authority..."*

Exciting new information

Visual Aid: Bring a yardstick with you.

Scripture: Mark 1:21-22

Here is some amazing, new information to tell you about. Did you know that a giraffe's tongue is 21 inches long, so long in fact, that it can wipe out its own eyes if something blows into them. And a giraffe can even wash out its own ears with its long tongue. WOW, new information can be so exciting!

Jesus had some new information for the people of his day that amazed them, too. "Jesus said to them, 'Do not judge, or you too will be judged.'" (Matt. 7:1), and then he said they were to be like the wise man who built his house on a rock (Matt. 7:24). These were things they had never heard before, not even from their own teachers.

The people were amazed! This was exciting, new information because Jesus taught them in a way different from what they were used to. He helped them understand the meaning of the words instead of just talking at them. So listen carefully when someone reads the Bible to you or when your teachers are telling you some new information. You may be amazed just like the people of Jesus' day were!

GENESIS 1:31

"God saw all that he had made, and it was very good..."

Dimples and dents 24

Visual Aid: Pass around an old golf ball.

Scripture: Genesis 1:31

Do you know what a golf ball looks like? It is small and round with dimples all over it. It isn't smooth or slick, it is dented. It is made that way because the dents in a golf ball make it go further when it is hit. For a long time, people used smooth round balls but then noticed that the used, dented ones went further. The perfect golf ball is not perfect at all.

Sometimes we might wish we hadn't been born the way we are. We want to look perfect! A nose might seem too long or too short, ears too large or too small, our toes might make our feet look funny. There are all kinds of things we wish we could change.

But WAIT. In Genesis, the first book in the Bible, God looks at all he has created and says it is GOOD. God created us, and He likes what He has made. When you think you want to change something about yourself, remember the golf ball. The dents make it so much better! God created you just right, just the way you are. There is a reason that the dented golf ball works better, and there is a reason we are the way we are.

ROMANS 8:35...

"Who shall separate us from the love of Christ?"

Stick with Jesus ◆25◆

Visual Aid: Use the frog picture in the Appendix, page 133, to copy.

Scripture: Romans 8:35...

Have you ever seen how a frog catches its food? A frog's tongue is very sticky, and when he catches a bug, the insect cannot get loose from that sticky tongue. If that tongue even barely touches the insect, old froggie will get his supper!

In the Bible, Romans 8:39 tells us about the love of God, which is in Christ Jesus. Like the bug on a frog's tongue cannot be taken away from the frog, the Bible says nothing in all creation will be able to take us away from the love of God that is in Christ Jesus our Lord. This means that we are to stick tightly to Jesus, and, because he loves us so much, he will stick tightly to us and we will NEVER be apart from his love!

What a wonderful promise—nothing in all creation will ever separate us from the love of God that we find in his son Jesus Christ. Whenever you feel lonely or sad, just remember that Jesus is with you, loves you, and will stick with you forever.

EXODUS 12:33

"*The Egyptians urged the people to hurry and leave the country...*"

Moving Van

Moving day 26

Visual Aid: Throw a paper airplane to focus attention.

Scripture: Exodus 12:33

Have any of you moved before? Good, then some of you know what it means to pack up, get ready, and, finally move. In this story of Moses and the Israelites (God's chosen people), millions of people all moved out of the land of Egypt on the same day to go into the new land that God had told them about. It took the people 40 years of travel before they finally arrived where God wanted them to be, and now God could bless them! The Israelites were given a new country and a new land to live in.

Sometimes when we move to a new place, we might be afraid, so we have to trust that God is going to take care of us and do something good for us in our new location. There are many different places to move to that might seem scary! This could be a new home, or a new school, or even a new family. But wherever we go, God is already there, so watch for your special something in the new place you move to.

Fall

JOHN 3:2

"He came to Jesus at night and said, 'Rabbi, we know that you are a teacher who has come from God...'"

Favorite teachers 27

Visual Aid: Hold up your old Bible.

Scripture: John 3:2

Almost everyone has had a favorite teacher—a schoolteacher, a Sunday School teacher, maybe a music teacher. The favorite teacher of the disciples in the Bible was God's own Son, Jesus.

These disciples didn't get summer vacation, and they never had time off from class because they were with their teacher all day, all night, and on weekends too! For three years, they followed Jesus around, learning all about him and what he had come into the world to do. They saw Jesus heal the sick and feed thousands of people, all the time teaching them about God.

These disciples were students just like you are today. They had lots of things to learn, so when their teacher, Jesus, was done teaching them, they would know about God, and they would know how to live and get along in the world.

Learning about God is a life-long adventure. As you study in school, remember also to study the Bible so you will know God and know how to live a good life.

JOHN 14:6

"Jesus said unto him,
'I am the way, the truth and the life;
no one comes to the Father except
through me.'"

Show and tell ◆28◆

Visual Aid: Show a picture of Jesus and a big red heart.

Scripture: John 14:6

How fun it is to tell your friends about something you really like or something you like to do, but when you get to show them, that makes it so much better! Show and tell makes it easier for others to understand what you are talking about.

For thousands of years, God tried to tell his people how to live and that he loved them, but the people did not understand what God was saying. So God sent his son Jesus to Earth, to be born, to walk, to talk, to laugh and play, to pray and care for others—to become a human being just like everyone else.

As Jesus grew up he told people of God's great love for them. Jesus healed the sick, taught them about God's kingdom in heaven, and then he showed them God's love for them, for all of us, by taking all the sins of the world and dying on a cross to save all people. This was God's greatest plan: to show his people how to live and that he loved them by giving us Jesus, who became the greatest Show and Tell anyone has ever seen!

GALATIANS 5:22-23

*"But the fruit of the Spirit
is love, joy, peace, forbearance,
kindness, goodness, faithfulness, gentleness,
and self-control."*

Who is your coach?

Visual Aid: Offer a plate of cookies and tell children to take only one cookie.

Scripture: Galatians 5:22-23

There are many different kinds of coaches: football, soccer, and baseball coaches. There are math coaches and music coaches. One thing they all have in common though, is that a good coach cares about you and will help you get better at what you are trying to do.

When Jesus went to Heaven, he said he would ask his Father God to send us a coach to be with us forever, so God sent us the Holy Spirit. The Holy Spirit loves us, and he helps us grow in our understanding of who God and Jesus are. The Holy Spirit coaches us in love, joy, peace, patience, kindness, goodness, faithfulness, gentleness, and self-control. Our Holy Spirit Coach shows us joy in a sunny morning, patience when we have to wait for cookies to come out of the oven, and self-control when we only get to eat one cookie before dinner. The Holy Spirit is there to help us be better in everything we do, and he is the Best Coach at helping us know God!

JOHN 3:16 KJV

"For God so loved the world that He gave His only begotten Son, that whosoever believeth in Him shall not perish, but have everlasting life."

Love at the football game

Visual Aid: Make a poster of John 3:16 and ask someone to wave it around.

Scripture: John 3:16 KJV

The football season has arrived. High school football teams are facing off on the field, and the fans are yelling and waving signs for their favorite team to win. There is excitement in the air!

Every once in a while, at a sports game, there is a sign someone holds up in the audience that says "John 3:16." Do you know what that is all about? Someone in the crowd wants you to know how much God loves you! A Christian person is showing his faith in God during that game.

John 3:16 tells us of God's love for us. Jesus Christ is God's only begotten Son, and if we want to have everlasting life, we need to believe in Jesus. And someone in that crowd wants you to know that. Someone wants you to have everlasting life in Heaven!

What a wonderful surprise to find love at the football game. The next time you are watching a sporting event, look at the crowd and see if you can find a sign that tells you of God's love for you. Someday you could be that person in the crowd who waves a sign that says "John 3:16."

MATTHEW 5:13 NLT

"You are the salt of the earth. But what good is salt if it has lost its flavor?"

Popcorn is mighty good with salt

Visual Aid: Bring a shaker of salt to look at.

Scripture: Matthew 5:13 NLT

Popcorn with a dash of salt is a favorite snack for most people. Popcorn without salt is pretty dull, so we like to put that small sprinkle of salt on our popcorn!

Today's scripture says we are the salt of the earth, and since salt improves things (like popcorn), wherever we go, we are also to improve things. For example, a playground with no one on it is just a piece of dirt! When that same playground is full of kids however, there is laughing, running, jumping, skipping, and conversation going on. Big difference!

The many pieces of popcorn are like the many places where we find God's children, and since we are called the salt of the earth, we make the playground, the classroom, and even our backyard better places to be. It is amazing how happy people become when a child smiles at them. This is being salt. When you help a neighbor to carry their groceries, that is being salt; as you pick up litter that was blown into the yard, that too, is being salt. Anywhere you go, you can improve that place, like salt improves the flavor of popcorn. You are the salt of the earth!

"*But when the grain had sprouted and produced a crop then the tares also appeared.*"

Wheat and weeds 32

Visual Aid: Hold hands upright to demonstrate how the plants grew up side by side. Then as they are grown up, keep one hand straight up to show the good plant and with the other hand, bend the fingers down to show the tares. As Jesus explains the parable, toss the tares away, but keep wheat fingers upright and wiggle them up into heaven.

Scripture: Matthew 13:26 NKJV

If you have ever helped to pull weeds, you know that roots can get tangled up with each other, and sometimes good plants get pulled out with the weeds. Jesus tells this story about weeds and wheat.

A farmer planted his field with good wheat seeds and that night someone else planted weed seeds, called tares, in the same field. When both plants came up, the field workers asked the farmer if they should pull up the weeds, and the farmer said they should wait until the wheat was ready to harvest, then pull the tares up and throw them into the fire, but put the wheat safely into the barn.

Then Jesus explained this story to his disciples. The farmer is Jesus, the wheat are God's children, the tares are the sons of the evil one, and the field workers are the angels. When the time is right, the angels will gather the sons of the evil one (tares) and throw them into the fire. Then the angels will gather God's children all together and take them to Heaven. Let us be God's children so we will be gathered up into Heaven when the time is right!

"Come to me, all you who are weary and burdened, and I will give you rest. Take my yoke upon you and learn from me, for I am gentle and humble in heart, and you will find rest for your souls."

Working together 33

Visual Aid: Using a picture of oxen yoked together might clarify what a yoke is. See Appendix, page 134, to copy the yoked oxen.

Scripture: Matthew 11:28-29

In Jesus' time, oxen, which are like big strong cows, were used to pull very heavy loads. They were connected to each other with a wooden collar, called a yoke that made the oxen walk together. Every time the oxen worked, they pulled together, side by side, and that made it much easier to move heavy loads.

When Jesus talked to the people of his time, they understood his idea of being yoked together. They could see how it would help to share the load with someone who was strong and right there beside them. We read in Matthew 11:28-29, that Jesus told the people, "Come to me, all you who are weary and burdened, and I will give you rest. Take my yoke upon you and learn from me, for I am gentle and humble in heart, and you will find rest for your souls."

Jesus was talking about all the troubles that people carry around with them. He asked the people to tell him their problems and he would join them, and, like two oxen working together, they would find it much easier to handle their troubles.

JOSHUA 6:10

"But Joshua had commanded
the army, 'Do not give a war cry, do not
raise your voices, do not say a word until
the day I tell you to shout.
Then shout!'"

Quiet please! ◆ 34

Visual Aid: First, take children in a quiet walk around the sanctuary.

Scripture: Joshua 6:10

After Moses died, God gave his people a new leader named Joshua. Joshua was the captain of the army of Israel and believed in God with all his heart. God wanted to give Israel a beautiful new land, but the enemy city of Jericho was already there. So God told Joshua to capture the city and take over the land. However, Jericho had a high stone wall all around it.

God told Joshua to be strong and courageous, not to be afraid, and do what God told him to do, and Joshua could win the battle! Then God told Joshua to have his army, the priests who blew their trumpets, and all the rest of God's people walk around the city of Jericho one time each day for six days. On the seventh day, they would walk around the city seven times.

During all this time, everyone had to be quiet—no talking, no whispering, no noise at all was to come out of their mouths—until Joshua told them to shout, and then they would shout and the city walls would come tumbling down! It happened just as God said it would. The city of Jericho fell down, and God's people had their new land!

1 CORINTHIANS 3:16

*"Don't you know
that you yourselves are
God's temple..."*

What is a church?

Visual Aid: A finger play to show the children. This is the church; show children how to fold hands upside down so all fingers are interlocked (this is the church). Put up both index fingers for the steeple (here is the steeple). Turn hands upright with interlocked fingers wiggling and say, "open the door and see all God's people."

Scripture: 1 Corinthians 3:16

When I was growing up, I thought the church was the red brick building on the corner. The beautiful stained glass windows with pictures of Jesus made me think this was the church.

Most everyone thinks the building is the church, but the building is just that—a building, the place where church gets together. For you see, the church is really all God's people gathered together in worship. There is an old children's song that says, "we are the church together."

The people make up the church, not the building, so no matter where we gather—in homes or in schools, or outside under the trees—church is wherever God's people are found worshipping, singing praises, and praying to the Lord.

ECCLESIASTES 12:13

"Now all has been heard; here is the conclusion of the matter: Fear God and keep his commandments..."

What should we do now? 36

Visual Aid: Have cookies to share with each child.

Scripture: Ecclesiastes 12:13

Have you ever helped make cookies? There are steps to follow in making cookies. First, we get a big bowl, and then the measuring cups, flour, sugar, and eggs. Then we turn the oven on to the right temperature. So now what should we do? Follow the recipe!

Making cookies takes time, and we have to follow the directions carefully. Making cookies also helps us understand this scripture in the Old Testament. (Read it here.)

After everything has been heard, then we do what we know is right. And just like there are steps to making cookies, there are steps to being a good Christian. First, we listen to the teachers of the Bible (that is like gathering the ingredients). Then we decide what we are to do (that is like turning on the oven). Finally, we are told to follow God and keep his commandments. That is following the recipe. When we follow God, we will turn out right, just like following the cookie recipe will turn out good cookies.

ISAIAH, 42:20

"You have seen many things, but you pay no attention; your ears are open, but you do not listen."

Peek-A-Boo 37

Visual Aid: Show a favorite Bible story picture to the children.

Scripture: Isaiah, 42:20

While I was shopping for a birthday gift, I saw a beautiful painting with a deer and lots of trees behind it. When it came time to buy the painting, the cashier asked if I had seen the other deer that were hidden among the trees in this picture. I didn't see them. I had missed them completely!

This reminded me of the scripture in the Bible that says our eyes have seen many things but have not paid attention to what we are looking at, and our ears don't listen to what is being said. There are some wonderful stories in the Bible, like David and Goliath, Noah and the flood, Jonah and the whale, and Jesus walking on the water or healing a blind man.

There are so many things to learn from the Bible—good stories, great ideas, and comforting words to help you in life. Be sure to keep your eyes and ears open! Many more stories are there for you to enjoy and learn from.

JOHN 15:16

"You did not choose me,
but I chose you and appointed
you so that you might go
and bear fruit—fruit
that will last..."

I choose YOU ◆38◆

Visual Aid: If possible, bring a bag of fruit and let each child
pick one.

Scripture: John 15:16

When we pick a piece of fruit like a banana or an apple, we choose which one we want. The fruit doesn't choose us; it can't jump up and down and yell, pick me, pick me! Choosing a fruit can remind us of the scripture in John 15:16 when Jesus told his disciples: (read the verse).

Jesus has chosen you, in your school, your church, your home, and your neighborhood, to go and bear fruit. The fruit that Jesus was talking about will last forever. It is called the Fruits of the Spirit. These are love, joy, peace, patience, kindness, goodness, faithfulness, gentleness, and self-control. No one can take these away from us. When we have these fruits in our life, we are filled with God's Holy Spirit, and people around us will see we are different because Jesus himself has chosen us!

PSALM 119:105

"Your word is a lamp for my feet, a light on my path."

Lamps and flashlights

Visual Aid: Have a flashlight with you to turn on.

Scripture: Psalm 119:105

When you walk around in the dark, it is easy to stub your toe on something you didn't see, but when you have a flashlight to show you the way, you are able to walk knowing you won't trip or fall. That light is like a warning for your feet: "Watch Out, Don't Trip" it says, or "Don't Go That Way, It's Dangerous."

In Bible times, people used lamps to light their way just like we use a flashlight today. But, flashlight or lamp, the idea is still the same: a light shows you what is up ahead and keeps you from falling.

The Bible tells us that God's word is a lamp for our feet and a light on our path, so by following the light that God gives us, we won't trip nearly so much, and we won't get into trouble or go where there is danger. And at the end of that path, we will find a great reward! The Bible tells us this in Psalm 19:11, "By them your servant is warned; in keeping them there is great reward."

Winter

DEUTERONOMY 6:5

"Love the LORD your God with all your heart and with all your soul and with all your strength."

Why am I here? 40

Visual Aid: Make copies to pass out of the attached animal tracks found in the Appendix, page 135.

Scripture: Deuteronomy 6:5

After rain or snow in the neighborhood, you may see animal tracks. Maybe you will see squirrel tracks, the neighbor's cat tracks, or bird tracks. It looks like the animals know why they are here and where they are going; their tracks are clear and easy to see.

When God created the animals and plants, each one was given a reason to be here, and God said that it was good. When it seems like everything else has a place in the world, we may wonder *why are we here?* Many people have asked this question! For the answer, let's go to the Bible to hear what it says.

In the book of Deuteronomy 6:5, it says, "Love the Lord your God with all your heart and with all your soul and with all your strength."

That means you are to love God, not just when you feel like it, not only with your heart, but with everything you are. That is the reason God made us, that is the reason we are here!

MALACHI 3:6 NKJV

"For I am the LORD
I do not change..."

In God we trust 41

Visual Aid: Have a coin for each child to look at.

Scripture: Malachi 3:6 NKJV

You can ask for change for a dollar bill and you will get coins. You can wear shorts and a short-sleeved shirt when it is sunny and hot, but the weather could quickly change to cloudy and cold! There are all kinds of changes that go on in our lives. Some changes are confusing, like the weather.

Wouldn't you be excited to find out there is something that never changes, something you can count on to stay the same? God never changes, not ever, never, never ever. The Bible says in the Book of Malachi 3:6, "For I am the LORD, I do not change..." WOW, imagine that!

God can be trusted. He means what he says, and what he says he will do! So when God says he loves you, that love will never change; it is the same love today and every day, even as you grow up. Each time you see a coin or a dollar bill, notice what it says: In God We Trust. And remember that you can trust God to love you because his love will never change.

"*I call on you, my God,*
for you will answer me;
turn your ear to me and
hear my prayer."

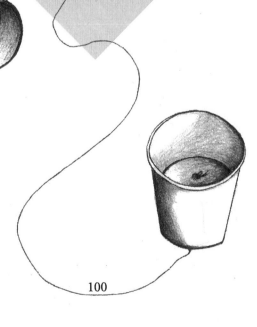

Can you hear me now?

Visual Aid: Make a "phone" by using two paper cups and string.
See Appendix, page 136, for instructions.

Scripture: Psalm 17:6

One day, two little boys were playing with two paper cups and a long piece of string. They put a hole in the bottom of each cup, put one end of the string into the hole and tied a knot at that end. They did the same thing for the other cup. Then they stood away from each other. One boy held a cup up to his ear, and the other boy spoke into his own cup. They called to each other as they went around the yard, behind trees, and around the corner of the house, yelling, "Can you hear me now?"

This was only a game for them; they wanted to be sure they were heard! But, if they were calling on God, they could be certain that God would hear them. God always hears his children.

If you're in the sunshine or in the dark, in the desert or in a park, God hears you. On a mountain or on the plain, in the snow or in the rain, God hears you. Wherever you're going, whatever you do, God always, always, listens to you. God loves you and listens for you to call on him!

"The baby's sister then stood at a distance watching to see what would happen to him [Moses]. Then the baby's sister approached the princess. 'Should I go and find one of the Hebrew women to nurse the baby for you?' she asked."

When only a child will do

Visual Aid: Hold up a basket and ask children what they might use a basket for.

Scripture: Exodus 2:4, 7 NLT

Baby Moses was born at a time when the King of Egypt ordered all Hebrew baby boys to be killed as soon as they were born! Little Moses was a Hebrew baby boy. Soon after he was born, his mother carefully hid him away to keep him safe. This was just fine for the first couple of months until little Moses started growing, then his mother made a waterproof basket and tucked Moses inside. She and big sister Miriam took the basket down to the Nile River and hid him in the weeds growing along the edge of the water.

Miriam stood watch over her little brother Moses to see what would happen to him, and pretty soon the King's sister, a princess, came by and saw the basket. The princess opened the basket and saw a little Hebrew baby boy, and she was worried. Up popped sister Miriam! God used a child to save the day. Miriam smiled and asked the princess if she wanted a Hebrew woman to nurse the baby for her. The princess was relieved. Miriam ran home and told her mother all that had happened, and now Moses' real mommy could still care for her own baby boy until she brought him back to the princess to raise as her own son.

Only a child could have saved Moses. If a grownup had talked to the princess, the princess would not have even listened. God knew that only a child could win the princess's heart to save baby Moses. So if you think that God can't use you because you are little, think again! God uses little children to do His will when adults just can't do it. God loves children. God loves you!

JOB 16:2

"*I have heard
many things like these;
you are miserable comforters,
all of you...*"

Encourage each other

Visual Aid: Ask two children to hold hands, suggesting they are friends.

Scripture: Job 16:2

A man in the Bible named Job had three friends who were not very good friends. When Job was having lots of trouble, these three men came to him and told him he must be guilty of some awful sin because they thought God was mad at him! But Job had not done anything wrong. These three men were not very good friends because they wouldn't believe Job, no matter what Job told them.

However, there was a reason for Job's troubles. God was using Job to remind others to have faith and trust in God even when things were going wrong. Job needed a good friend who would pray for him and help him remember that God would always be there to love and care for him.

A good friend helps us trust God even in the bad times. Do you have good friends? Find a good friend who will pray for you and encourage you when you have troubles. Are you a good friend to other people? Remember Job, and when your friends are having a hard time, pray for them and bring them comfort and encouraging words to help them trust in God until they get back to happier times.

ROMANS 12:2 NLT

"Don't copy the behavior and customs of this world, but let God transform you into a new person by changing the way you think."

Don't be a copy cat 45

Visual Aid: If possible, have one original picture and a smeared or fuzzy copy of it.

Scripture: Romans 12:2 NLT

When copies are made, it is best to use the original picture or writing because copies are usually fuzzy around the edges and not as clear or sharp as the original.

God wants us to be original, new and fresh, not a copy of how someone else behaves or acts. We are to be the people God made us to be and grow up as He has designed us to grow.

The Bible says we all have been given certain things that we do well. These are the things that God wants us to work on to make them even better! We are to be that new, fresh person who gets sharper and clearer all the time, not like a copy that is fuzzy and dull. Stay true to who you are; be the best person you can be!

GENESIS 45:8

Joseph said, "So then, it was not you who sent me here, but God. He made me father to Pharaoh, lord of his entire household and ruler of all Egypt."

Joseph—God's man!

Visual Aid: Find a picture of ancient Egyptian noblemen or copy the Joseph drawing from the Appendix, page 137.

Scripture: Genesis 45:8

This verse in Genesis talks about Joseph, who was only a teenager when his brothers sold him as a slave. Joseph ended up becoming a very important man in Egypt. Many years later when these same brothers traveled to Egypt, Joseph welcomed them!

Joseph realized that his brothers who had sold him were only doing God's will. Now, these same brothers had come to ask for food since there had been no rain in their land and everything was dying. Even before his brothers came to Egypt, Joseph had been warned by God to have lots of food stored up. Then, when the fields dried up and there was no food, Joseph's brothers and their families were able to come to Egypt to find food and safety.

God works in our lives to prepare us for what is coming later. There will be times when you will have problems, but wait, God is working in your life, getting you ready for tomorrow! Remember, God cared for Joseph, and God cares for you!

MATTHEW 10:30

"And even the very hairs of your head are all numbered."

Even the smallest things

Visual Aid: Have a hairbrush on your lap and pull out a hair from it as you talk.

Scripture: Matthew 10:30

When I went to the barber shop this week to get my hair cut, the barber cut off so much that it made me wonder if there was any hair left on my head. I didn't know how that haircut would turn out. But God knew!

The Bible tells us that God even knows how many hairs are on our head. God knows the smallest things about us, so we can trust that He cares about the big things that happen to us, too. We cannot always figure out what God is doing because He often works behind the scenes. This is called Providence. Providence means that God is in control of everything that happens to us even if we can't see it!

There will be times in life when you can't imagine how anything good can come of what has happened to you. That is the time to remember that God loves and cares about you and to trust that God knows what he is doing. We don't need to know how or why things are happening as they are. We just need to trust that God is in control.

ROMANS 12:4

"For just as each of us has one body with many members, and these members do not all have the same function,"

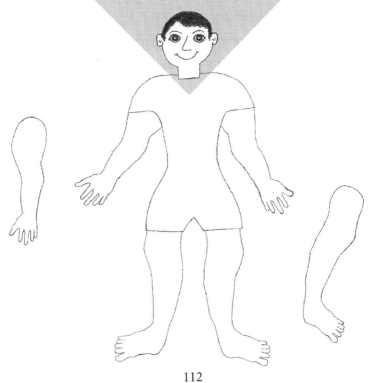

Special You! 48

Visual Aid: Use paper cut outs found in the Appendix, page 138, and attach the parts together with brads.

Scripture: Romans 12:4

Our friends do many different things, don't they? One friend may sing, one may enjoy drawing, while another one listens carefully, and still another friend might be helpful and kind. We like to do the things we are good at, don't we? This is because God has put some special thing, some talent, inside each of us. This is a gift from God, and it makes each one of us special!

Today's scripture (read it here) tells us that our bodies have many parts, and all these together make up only one body. And so it is with Jesus Christ. Many parts make up only one body, called the body of Jesus Christ. For example, the friend who likes to draw could be the hands of Jesus, the friend who always listens to others could be like Jesus' ears, and the friend who sings might be like Jesus' what? (point to your mouth and encourage someone to connect this talent to Jesus' mouth).

Each one of us is part of Christ's body: we do the work of his arms, his legs, his hands and feet, his voice and his heart of love; for each of us is a special part of the body of Christ!

EXODUS 31:8-11

"...the table and its articles,
the pure gold lampstand and all its
accessories, the altar of incense, the altar
of burnt offering and all its utensils,
the basin with its stand and
also the woven garments, both
the sacred garments for Aaron the priest
and the garments for his sons when they
serve as priests, and the anointing
oil and fragrant incense for
the Holy Place."

That reminds me... 49

Visual Aid: Refer to a candle stand or another altar item close by.

Scripture: Exodus 31:8-11

When you first go into church, you may see stained glass windows, a large cross, an altar, candles, perhaps a piano or organ. All these things help remind you that this is God's house, the church. Now, look around you and what else do you see? (Encourage children to name what they see in their church.)

In church as it was in the temple of Bible times, there are some things that we don't normally see. That is because the church is called God's house and it looks a little different than your house.

When you go outside, what do you see there? Trees, birds, clouds and sky, perhaps flowers in the summer, or snow in the winter. These things also remind us of God.

Inside our church, we see things that make it special and beautiful; outside we still see many things that make our world beautiful. So, whether inside or outside, we are reminded that God is everywhere!

"For unto us a Child is born, unto us a Son is given; and the government will be upon His shoulder. And His name will be called Wonderful, Counselor, Mighty God, Everlasting Father, Prince of Peace."

Christmas Boxes 50

Visual Aid: Have two Christmas gifts wrapped and ready to open.

Scripture: Isaiah 9:6 NKJV

To begin this lesson, have two very nicely wrapped boxes sitting in your lap, one box with underwear in it and the other box with socks in it. Allow the children to hold the boxes, to guess what might be in them, and build excitement as to what might be in these gifts. Notice the wrapping, ribbons or bows, shake the boxes. When the children are very excited about the presents, have a child unwrap one. Is the child disappointed when he pulls out the socks or underwear?

Ask, "Was this expected?" NO! "Are you disappointed?" YES! "This certainly was not what we had hoped for! But there is another box, certainly this one will be better!" Again, grow the excitement going through the same motions. Ask another child to open this present, and act very disappointed as this child pulls out the other item. Ask, "Are you disappointed with this present? Yes." Tell the children you can understand how disappointed they are.

There is however, one gift that will never disappoint you! That one is Jesus Christ, God's only Son, who came to us as the first Christmas gift. Some things you get on Christmas might be disappointing; they will not be what was hoped for or asked for. But the gift of the Son of God will never, ever, never disappoint. It is God's love all wrapped up in the gift of the baby Jesus.

"When someone becomes a Christian, he becomes a brand new person inside. He is not the same anymore. A new life has begun!"

What's new with you? 51

Visual Aid: Show an illustration or photo of a butterfly and a
                cocoon.

Scripture: 2 Corinthians 5:17 TLB

Last summer in the garden, a small caterpillar wrapped itself up
in silk threads that made a cover all around its body called a
cocoon. After a few weeks, the cocoon opened up, and SURPRISE,
a butterfly came out!

The caterpillar had changed into a beautiful butterfly; now it
was a whole new creature with wings, long legs, and big eyes—no
longer a tiny little caterpillar! This is a reminder that when we
accept Jesus as our Savior, we change, too (read scripture here).
Like the caterpillar that changed into a butterfly and began a new
life, we too, can change and start a new life as a Christian! Just like
the scripture says, "A new life has begun."

What a great way to begin the New Year! If you haven't already
asked Jesus to be your Savior and come into your heart, this is the
perfect time to do it. You, too, can be a new creature and start a
wonderful new life as a Christian with Jesus Christ, the one who
loves you more than anything! Happy New Year!

LUKE 24:51

"While he was blessing them, he left them and was taken up into heaven."

He is coming again! 52

Visual Aid: Watch Jesus going up into a heavenly cloud cup.
See Appendix, page 139, for directions.

Scripture: Luke 24:51

Often during a holiday, airplanes roar through the skies high above us. When we hear them, we usually look up to see what kind of plane is making all that noise, and while we can't always see the airplane because of the clouds, we know it is there! When we do get to see the airplane, it is fun to watch it get smaller and smaller until…POOF! it disappears.

The disciples were listening to Jesus talk to them, and after blessing them, Jesus began to rise up into the clouds until poof! he disappeared. They watched until they could no longer see Jesus, but the disciples knew he was still there.

While they were looking up toward heaven, two men dressed in white robes appeared and stood beside them. These men asked the disciples why they were looking up into heaven. The men said that Jesus would come back one day, the same way the disciples saw him go.

So, just like an airplane will come back to earth, Jesus will one day come back to earth too! That is a promise from the Bible.

Appendix
Lesson Visual Aids

Lesson 2 Visual Aid

Copy the sparrow picture for each child.

Lesson 3
Visual Aid

Copy the attached picture of a whale. Cut out and slice along the line in the center of the whale's body. On the back of the picture, glue a strip of paper on three sides and paste over the slice with the unglued edge up. Move Jonah in and out of the whale or keep him in place as needed.

Lesson 6 Visual Aid

Copy the hen and chicks picture for each child.

Lesson 7 Visual Aid

Copy and cut out both hearts with scriptures. Glue them back to back over a straw. Twist the straw to illustrate the three times that Jesus asked, "Do you love me?" and Peter's response on the other side.

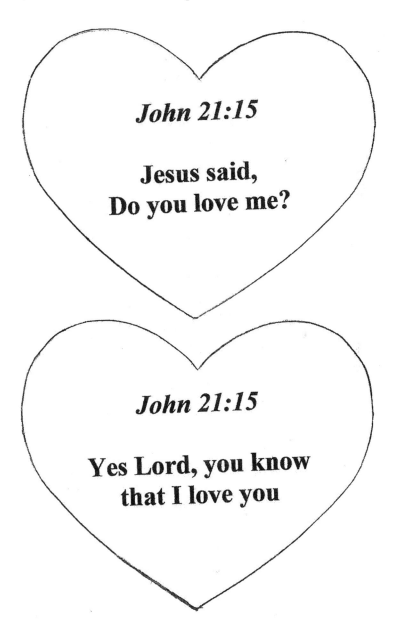

John 21:15

**Jesus said,
Do you love me?**

John 21:15

**Yes Lord, you know
that I love you**

Lesson 8 Visual Aid

Copy the elephant picture for each child.

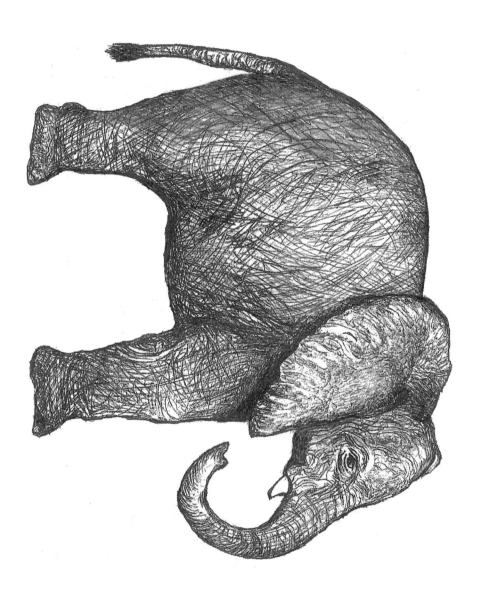

Lesson 11 Visual Aid

Soft clay recipe:

1 cup flour
½ cup salt
2 tsp. cream of tarter

1 cup water
2 Tbls of cooking oil
Several drops of food coloring

Mix all ingredients together in a saucepan until smooth. Cook over low heat stirring constantly until mixture forms a smooth ball. Take soft ball and kneed it until slightly cooled. Store in an air-tight container to keep it soft.

Lesson 13 Visual Aid

Copy the picture of feet for each child.

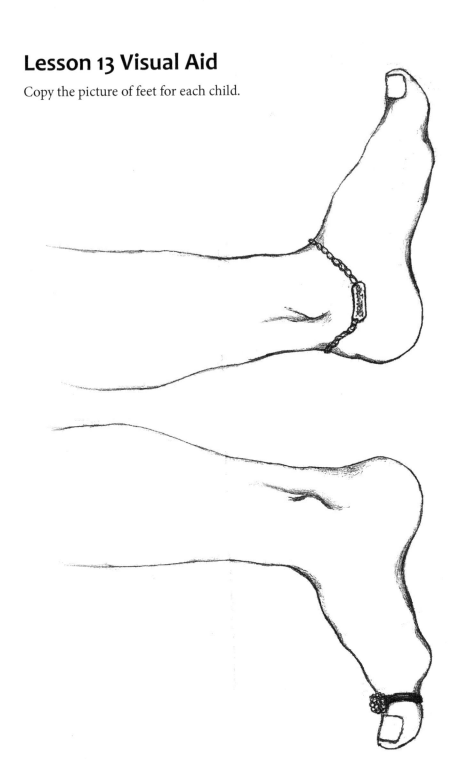

Lesson 15 Visual Aid

Directions to make a plastic bag parachute:

Take a plastic bag without rips or tears. Cut off the handles at one end and the bottom at the other end. Then unfold it and cut off the excess to make a perfect square. Using a large bowl, lay the bowl upside down on the plastic and cut a circle. you should have a reasonably round circle of plastic. Now make 6 dots around the edge of the circle, equal distance from each other. Place a piece of invisible tape over each dot and, using a needle, make a hole through the tape and the plastic. The tape strengthens the holes.

Using lightweight string, measure 1½ times the distance from edge to edge of the circle, and cut six strings of equal length. Thread an end of each string through a hole, tie it at the hole leaving the rest of the string hanging.

Gather all the strings together and tie a knot using the ends of all six strings so the strings are approximately the same length from plastic to knot. Take a small nut and bolt and attach it onto the knot of six strings. Lift the parachute at the center and throw it up into the air or drop it over a staircase and watch it float down. If the parachute is lopsided or doesn't float well, notice this. Remember that God, like a perfectly packed parachute, can be trusted not to fail.

Lesson 19 Visual Aid

Directions to make a puzzle:

Using a heavy card stock, copy the puzzle picture below onto it.

Now, glue a picture onto the other side of the puzzle. Then cut out along the puzzle piece lines to make your own puzzle.

Lesson 25 Visual Aid

Copy the picture of a frog for each child.

Lesson 33 Visual Aid

Copy the picture of yoked oxen for each child.

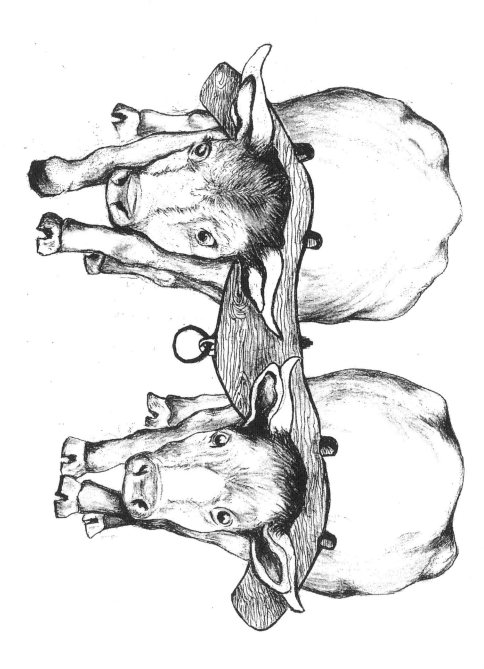

Lesson 40 Visual Aid

Copy the picture of animal tracks for each child.

Lesson 42 Visual Aid

Directions to make a cup and string "phone":

You will need 2 small paper cups and a piece of string long enough so that two children can hold each end and talk on the phone. Using a needle, make a hole in the bottom of each paper cup.

Thread an end of the string from the outside through the the hole into the bottom of each cup. Tie a knot in each end so the string is secured.

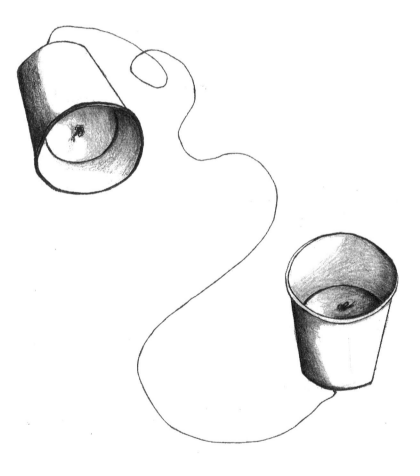

Lesson 46 Visual Aid

Copy the picture of Joseph.

Lesson 48 Visual Aid

Instructions:

If you would like, enlarge the parts illustration to double. Cut the pieces out and using brads, join at the dots. You will be able to move the body parts as you tell the story for a more interesting visual aid for your presentation.

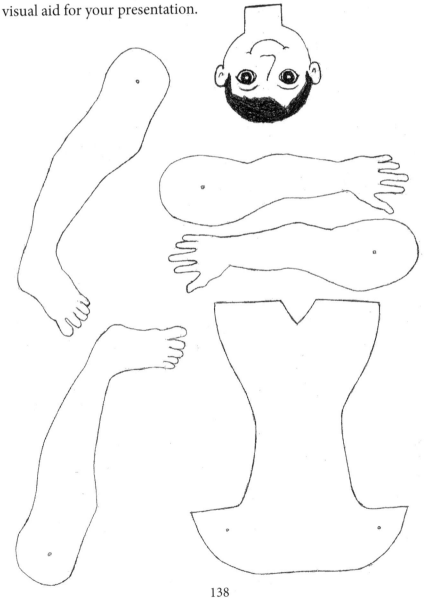

Lesson 52 Visual Aid

Cloud Cup directions:

Take a paper cup and glue cotton balls or white paper "clouds" all around the cup. Then punch a small hole in the bottom of the paper cup. Thread string through the cup and glue a picture of Jesus, or a small figurine, onto the other end of the string. Pull the string up through the hole as Jesus goes up into the clouds. Have Jesus come back to earth by pulling little Jesus back down from the clouds!

About the Author

Gretchen Arnold has always held a special place in her heart for children and for over 30 years, she has told them Bible stories during the Children's Sunday Sermon time at her local United Methodist Church. A life-long resident of Colorado Springs, CO, she has led many Vacation Bible School groups, taught Sunday School to children and adults, and designed and led preschool nature programs at a local nature center.

Gretchen has been honored with awards from her church, and was nominated in 1992 as Colorado Springs Woman of the Year.

After retirement, she felt it was time to compile her favorite children's Sunday sermons to share with teachers, parents, and group leaders who are looking for a way to help children find God, but don't have much time at the end of a long work day to create a lesson. Gretchen offers this book as their guide.

Additional copies of

A Collection of Sunday Sermons for Children

by Gretchen Arnold

are available by ordering online at

amazon.com

(search for "Gretchen Arnold")

Made in the USA
Middletown, DE
02 January 2025

68702330R00080